The Ultimate Harry Styles Fan Book

100+ Facts, Quiz, Photos + More

Jamie Anderson

BELLANOVA

MELBOURNE · SOFIA · BERLIN

Contents

Harry Styles
INTRODUCTION

Since auditioning for X-Factor in 2010, Harry Styles has taken over the pop world. First as a member of One Direction, and then as a just-as-awesome solo star.

So how much do you *really* know about Harry? In this book you will learn about Harry's career, what his childhood was like and much more. Are you ready? *Let's go!*

Harry Styles FUN FACTS

Harry's hair wasn't always curly! It was straight until the end of primary school.

• • •

Harry has four nipples! As well as his normal two, he has two extra tiny ones.

• • •

Harry came up with the name One Direction for the band during The X-Factor.

Before The X-Factor, Harry applied for a job as a lifeguard.

• • •

Harry apparently calls his mom up to five times a day. He's a big mommy's boy!

• • •

Harry often talks in his sleep.

• • •

Harry is really good friends with fellow British pop star, Ed Sheeran.

I think you have to take me for me. I am who I am."

– Harry Styles

Harry said he used to pole dance in the schoolyard when he was younger.

• • •

When Harry first signed up for Instagram, the handle @HarryStyles was taken, so he created a profile with @GiveMeMyNamePlease and the owner was kind enough to give it to him.

• • •

Harry had the most solo parts on One Direction's debut album.

Harry once shaved his own initials into Zayn's leg!

• • •

Harry used to be so nervous about performing that he'd be sick before going on stage.

• • •

Some of Harry's nicknames are Hazza, Haz, Curly, and Harold.

• • •

Harry's father is Jewish and his mother is Roman Catholic.

Be a lover. Give love. Choose love. Love everyone, always."

– Harry Styles

Harry is very ticklish!

• • •

Harry's favourite album is *Astral Weeks* by Van Morrison.

• • •

When Harry released his album *Fine Lines*, it had the highest first-week sales by a British male act in the United States.

• • •

In July 2020, Harry Styles narrated a bedtime story for the *Calm* app, called *Dream with me*.

Harry wrote most of his album *'Harry Styles'* in Jamaica.

• • •

Harry once spent a day handing out pizzas to homeless people in Los Angeles.

• • •

Harry's former boss at the bakery he worked at said that Harry was the most polite member of staff he had ever had!

In his first school play, Harry played a mouse called Barney.

• • •

Harry and Ed Sheeran have matching tattoos.

• • •

Although Harry is known for his love of parties, he spent his 25th birthday reading in a coffeeshop in Japan!

• • •

Harry used to record song covers on his granddad's karaoke machine.

Harry Styles
Quiz: Family & Early Life

From where Harry was born, to his parents names — how much do you know about Harry before he was famous?

1   What are Harry's parents' names?

• • •

2   Where was Harry born?

3   What was Harry's first girlfriend's name?

• • •

4   When was Harry born?

• • •

5   What is Harry's middle name?

• • •

6   Where did Harry grow up?

• • •

7   What band was Harry in before he became famous on the X-Factor?

8 Where did Harry work part-time before the X-Factor?

• • •

9 What was the first gig that Harry ever attended?

• • •

10 What was Harry's pet hamster called?

• • •

11 What was the name of Harry's pre-school?

"

"I'd like to take care of someone but at the same time, I like girls who are independent."

– Harry Styles

12   What was Harry's nickname at school?

• • •

13   What was Harry's first pet?

• • •

14   What is Harry's sister called?

• • •

15   What secondary (high) school did Harry attend?

16 What was Harry's first word?

• • •

17 What type of animal attacked him when he was 10?

• • •

18 What is Harry's full first name?

• • •

19 What colour was Harry's hair when he was born?

20 When did Harry's parents get divorced?

• • •

21 What was the first song Harry learned all the words to?

• • •

22 How tall is Harry?

• • •

23 What colour are Harry's eyes?

ANSWERS

How many did you get right?

1. His mum is called Anne Cox and his dad is Des Styles.
2. Evesham, Worcestershire in England.
3. Emilie. They started dating when he was 12.
4. 1 February, 1994.
5. Edward.
6. Holmes Chapel in Cheshire, England.
7. He was the lead singer of White Eskimo.
8. W Mandeville bakery in Cheshire.
9. Nickleback, in Manchester.
10. Hamster!
11. Happy Days.
12. Hazza.

13. A dog called Max.
14. Gemma.
15. Holmes Chapel Comprehensive School.
16. Cat.
17. A goat! Luckily he survived to tell the tale.
18. Harold.
19. Bright blonde!
20. When he was seven.
21. 'The Girl of My Best Friend' by Elvis Presley.
22. Harry is 6 ft (183 cm) tall.
23. Green.

Harry Styles QUIZ: MUSIC & CAREER

1   Who are some of Harry's main musical heroes?

• • •

2   What did Harry sing during the first round of the X-Factor?

3 What is the name of the song that Harry wrote for Ariana Grande?

• • •

4 What 2017 movie did Harry act in?

• • •

5 What was the first single released from Harry's second album, *Fine Line*?

• • •

6 Which actress will Harry star opposite in the new film *Don't Worry Darling*?

7 What was Harry's first solo single, and what year was it released?

• • •

8 What three singles did Harry release from his album *Harry Styles*?

• • •

9 How many Grammy awards has Harry been nominated for, and how many has he won?

Eating toast in the shower is the ultimate multitask."

– Harry Styles

10 What was Harry's first number-one single in the USA?

• • •

11 How many BRIT Awards has Harry won?

• • •

12 On which continents did Harry perform during his *Harry Styles: Live on Tour* tour in 2017-18?

• • •

13 What award did Harry win at the 2020 *American Music Awards*?

14 When did One Direction announce they were going on hiatus?

• • •

15 When did Harry host *Saturday Night Live* for the first time?

• • •

16 Which famous actor did Harry replace in the film *Don't Worry Darling*?

• • •

17 Harry wrote a song with Meghan Trainor called '*Someday*'. Who's album did it appear on?

I think when you're writing songs, it's impossible to not draw on personal experiences, whether it be traveling or girls, or anything."

– Harry Styles

18 Which fashion designer did Harry become the face of in 2018?

• • •

19 Harry was the first man to appear on the cover of which magazine?

• • •

20 What is the name of Harry's 2021 tour?

• • •

21 Who is the supporting act for most dates on Harry's 2021 tour?

ANSWERS

How many did you get right?

1. The Beatles, Elvis and Coldplay.
2. Stevie wonder's 'isn't she lovely'
3. Just a Little Bit Of Your Heart, from her My Everything album.
4. Dunkirk.
5. Lights Up.
6. Olivia Wilde.
7. Sign of the Times, in 2017.
8. Sign of the Times, Two Ghosts and Kiwi.
9. One win (Best Pop Vocal Performance, Watermelon Sugar) out of three nominations.
10. Watermelon Sugar.
11. Two.

12. North and South Americas, Europe, Asia, and Australia
13. Favorite Pop/Rock Album for Fine Line.
14. January 2016.
15. In 2019.
16. Shia LaBouef.
17. Michael Bublé.
18. Gucci.
19. Vogue.
20. Love on Tour 2021.
21. Jenny Lewis.

Harry Styles
QUIZ: PRIVATE LIFE

Harry has featured in many gossip magazines over the years, usually because of his celebrity relationships! From Taylor Swift to Caroline Flack, Harry is always keeping things interesting.

1   Harry sparked controversy when he started dating Caroline Flack in 2011. What was their age difference?

2 When did Harry have his first kiss?

• • •

3 What illness does Harry suffer from?

• • •

4 Which member of the Kardashian-Jenner family did Harry date in 2013?

• • •

5 Which Victoria's Secret model, which Harry dated, inspired his album *Fine Line*?

6 What diet has Harry been following since 2017?

• • •

7 In what year did Harry date Taylor Swift?

• • •

8 Which Taylor Swift songs are believed to have been written about Harry?

• • •

9 Where does Harry live?

Age is just a number, maturity is a choice."

– Harry Styles

10 How much is Harry estimated to be worth in 2021?

• • •

11 Who did Harry endorse in the 2020 US presidential election, despite being unable to vote?

• • •

12 Who is Harry currently dating (2021)?

• • •

13 Who was Harry's first love, when he was 15?

14 How much money did Harry raise for charity during his 2017 tour?

• • •

15 Harry and Taylor were photographed going on a date in which park?

• • •

16 How many followers does Harry have on Instagram (August 2021)?

ANSWERS

How many did you get right?

1. 14 years.
2. When he was 11.
3. Hayfever.
4. Kendall Jenner.
5. Camille Rowe.
6. Pescatarian, meaning he only eats fish (no other meat).
7. 2012-2013.
8. I Knew You Were Trouble, Out of the Woods and Style.
9. In North London.

10. £75 million.
11. Joe Biden.
12. Olivia Wilde.
13. Felicity Skinner.
14. $1.2 million.
15. Central Park, New York.
16. 39 million.

Harry Styles
THE LYRIC QUIZ

Can you name which songs these lyrics are from?

1 "Trying to remember what it feels like to have a heartbeat"

2 "Even my phone misses your call."

3 "Don't you call him/her what you used to call me"

4 "All the lights couldn't put out the dark"

5 "I want your belly and that summer feelin'"

6 "Do you think it's easy / Being of the jealous kind?"

7 "Wherever I go, you bring me home"

8 "You can't bribe the door on your way to the sky"

9 "Brooklyn saw me, empty at the news / There's no water inside this swimming pool"

10 "And I can't take it back, I can't unpack the baggage you left"

11 "Maybe, we can find a place to feel good"

12 "I walked the streets all day / Running with the thieves"

13 "She's driving me crazy, but I'm into it"

14 "She lives in daydreams with me / She's the first one that I see"

15 "Walk in your rainbow paradise / Strawberry lipstick state of mind"

ANSWERS

How many did you get right?

1. Two Ghosts.
2. The Dining Table.
3. Cherry.
4. Lights Up.
5. Watermelon Sugar.
6. To Be So Lonely.
7. Sweet Creature.
8. Sign of the Times.
9. Ever Since New York.
10. Falling.
11. Treat people with kindness.
12. Meet Me in the Hallway.
13. Kiwi.
14. She.
15. Adore You.

Harry Styles
BONUS QUIZ

Now it's time to test your knowledge on the most random Harry Styles facts. It's going to be tough, so good luck!

1 What is Harry's Twitter handle?

2 What is Harry's favorite song of all time?

3 What did Harry want to be if he wasn't a pop star?

4   What football team does Harry support?

5   What are Harry's favourite colors?

6   Harry has admitted to loving 'chick flicks'. What are his favourites?

7   What shoe size is Harry?

8   What sports does Harry like to play?

9   What is Harry's favorite animal?

16   Does Harry wear boxers or briefs?

17   What was Harry's first tattoo?

18   What small instrument can Harry play?

19   Does Harry prefer tea or coffee?

20   Which Disney character did Harry say he'd most like to be?

ANSWERS

How many did you get right?

1. @harry_styles
2. 'FREE FALLING' BY JOHN MAYER
3. A physiotherapist.
4. Manchester United.
5. Orange and blue.
6. Love Actually, Titanic and The Notebook.
7. Size 10 (UK).
8. Tennis, badminton and golf.
9. Turtles.
10. The ability to travel through time.
11. Family Guy.
12. Apple juice.
13. Ophidiophobia — a fear of snakes.
14. 'Work hard, play hard, be kind.'
15. Aquarius.
16. Boxers.
17. A star - he said each point of the star represented a member of one direction.
18. The kazoo.
19. He much prefers tea.
20. Sebastian the crab from The Little Mermaid.

Harry Styles QUOTES

Harry has always been the funny guy in One Direction — he's always making us giggle! But, he can also be smart and inspiring.

These are some of our favourite Harry Styles quotes — funny and serious!

"A real girl isn't perfect and a perfect girl isn't real."

• • •

"My first real crush was... Louis Tomlinson."

• • •

"It only takes a second for you to call a girl fat and she will starve herself for the rest of her life. Think before you act."

• • •

"A dream is only a dream.. until you decide to make it real."

"I feel like I've woken up with suddenly more facial hair and a deeper voice."

• • •

"I hate the word famous because it has no substance."

• • •

"People often ask me why don't you have a girlfriend. Then I smile and say: I have thousands some just haven't met me yet."

"A lot of the time, the way it's portrayed is that I only see women in a sexual way. But I grew up with just my mum and sister, so I respect women a lot."

• • •

"I'm quite old-fashioned. I like going out to dinner. You have the chance to talk to somebody and get to know them better."

• • •

"I like girls who have two eyes."

"Quite a lot of the girls I get photographed with are just friends and then, according to the papers I have, like, 7,000 girlfriends."

• • •

"Tall girls are hot. Short girls are cute."

• • •

"I've got four nipples. I think I must have been a twin, but the one other went away and left its nipples behind."

"

I love anything that's a bit of a challenge."

– Harry Styles

"I find ambition really attractive too – if someone's good at something they love doing. I want someone who is driven."

. . .

"I think you should not be scared of embarrassing yourself, I think it builds character."

. . .

"I've always wanted to be one of those people who didn't really care much about what people thought about them... but I don't think I am."

Harry Styles
WORDSEARCH

Q	F	P	I	Q	W	Z	X	C	V	F	D
B	A	Z	X	X	V	M	U	S	I	C	G
V	L	C	V	R	F	E	S	O	I	U	F
C	L	Y	H	T	Y	A	Z	X	C	G	F
P	I	T	A	A	B	G	C	U	Y	R	I
O	N	E	D	I	R	E	C	T	I	O	N
E	G	S	O	J	H	R	N	B	O	V	E
W	B	D	R	V	Z	X	Y	N	B	R	L
A	V	F	E	N	G	L	A	N	D	M	I
N	Q	W	Y	J	H	G	F	D	S	N	N
B	R	E	O	C	K	I	W	I	B	V	E
V	X	Z	U	Q	W	E	H	G	D	A	C

Can you find all the words below in the wordsearch puzzle on the left?

HARRY   ONE DIRECTION   FALLING

FINE LINE   ADORE YOU   X FACTOR

MUSIC   ENGLAND   KIWI

Harry Styles
CROSSWORD PUZZLE

Answer the clues and fill in the puzzle —good luck!

Across

1. Middle name.
5. Show that made him famous.
7. Type of shop he first worked in.
8. Second album.
9. Second solo single.

Down

2. First movie he acted in.
3. Sister's name.
4. First band.
6. Starsign.

We hope you learnt some awesome facts about Harry!

What was your favourite? How did you do in the quiz? Let us know in a review on Amazon —we'd love to hear from you!

Manufactured by Amazon.ca
Bolton, ON

27893486R00045